GW01158197

Bible Adventures for Little Hearts

The Miracles of Jesus

Ages 3-5   Vol 2

Paul Devine

Phil 4:13 I can do all things through Christ which strengtheneth me.

Unless otherwise noted, all Scripture quotations are taken from the (Authorized 1611 King James Version).

This book is designed to teach young minds a few of Jesus' miracles and the lives he touched. Each occasion has a fun coloring page following the brief lesson.

ISBN: 979-8-3484-9893-1

Table of Contents

Jesus Turns Water Into Wine

Story:

Jesus and His mother, Mary, went to a wedding in Cana. The party was going well, but soon the wine ran out. Mary told Jesus, "They have no wine." Jesus asked the servants to fill six big jars with water.

After they filled the jars, Jesus told them to pour some out and give it to the man in charge. When they did, the water had turned into wine—wonderful wine! The man in charge of the party was surprised and said, "This is the best wine!"

This was Jesus' first miracle. It showed His power and care for others. His disciples saw what He did and believed in Him. Isn't it amazing how Jesus can do things no one else can?

The guests at the wedding didn't know where the wine had come from, but they were overjoyed by how delicious it was. The servants, who had seen what happened, were amazed by Jesus' power. This miracle wasn't just about wine—it showed how much Jesus cares about our needs.

Scripture:

"This beginning of miracles did Jesus in Cana of Galilee, and manifested forth his glory; and his disciples believed on him." – John 2:11

Questions:

- What did Jesus turn the water into?
- How many jars did the servants fill?
- How did Jesus' disciples feel after seeing this miracle?

Phil 4:13 I can do all things through Christ which strengtheneth me.

Phil 4:13 I can do all things through Christ which strengtheneth me.

Jesus Feeds 5,000 People

Story:

One day, a huge crowd of over 5,000 people followed Jesus to hear Him teach. They stayed all day, and by evening, everyone was hungry. The disciples told Jesus, "We don't have enough food for all these people!"

Then a boy brought his small lunch—five loaves of bread and two fish. Jesus took the food, looked up to heaven, and thanked God. He broke the bread and fish into pieces and gave it to His disciples to pass out. The amazing thing was, the food didn't run out!

Everyone ate until they were full, and when they were done, the disciples collected twelve baskets of leftovers. Jesus had done another miracle, showing His power and love to care for people's needs.

The crowd couldn't believe their eyes as the food kept coming. Families smiled and shared with one another, amazed at Jesus' kindness and power. The little boy who shared his lunch must have been so happy to see how Jesus used his small gift to bless so many people.

Scripture:

"And they did all eat, and were filled: and they took up of the fragments that remained twelve baskets full." – Matthew 14:20

Questions:

- How many loaves of bread and fish did the boy bring to Jesus?
- Who made the food enough for everyone to eat?
- How many baskets of leftovers were collected?

Phil 4:13 I can do all things through Christ which strengtheneth me.

Phil 4:13 I can do all things through Christ which strengtheneth me.

Jesus Walks on Water

Story:

One evening, Jesus sent His disciples across the sea in a boat while He stayed behind to pray. As they rowed, the wind became strong, and the waves grew high. The disciples struggled against the storm, feeling scared and tired.

Early in the morning, Jesus came to them, walking on the water! The disciples saw Him and were afraid because they thought He was a ghost. But Jesus called out, "Be of good cheer; it is I; be not afraid."

Peter said, "Lord, if it's really You, let me walk to You on the water." Jesus said, "Come." Peter stepped out of the boat and started walking on the water too! But when Peter saw the big waves, he became afraid and began to sink. He cried, "Lord, save me!" Jesus reached out His hand and caught him.

When they climbed into the boat, the wind stopped. The disciples worshipped Jesus, saying, "Truly, You are the Son of God."

Scripture:

"But straightway Jesus spake unto them, saying, Be of good cheer; it is I; be not afraid." – Matthew 14:27

Questions:

- Who walked on the water first?
- What happened when Peter became afraid?
- What did the disciples say about Jesus after the wind stopped?

Phil 4:13 I can do all things through Christ which strengtheneth me.

Phil 4:13 I can do all things through Christ which strengtheneth me.

Jesus Calms the Storm

Story:

One day, Jesus and His disciples got into a boat to cross the sea. Jesus was tired and went to sleep at the back of the boat. Suddenly, a fierce storm came, with big waves crashing into the boat. The disciples were scared that they would sink.

They woke Jesus and said, "Master, don't You care that we are about to drown?" Jesus stood up and said to the wind and the waves, "Peace, be still." Immediately, the wind stopped, and the sea became calm.

Jesus turned to His disciples and said, "Why are you so afraid? Where is your faith?" The disciples were amazed and whispered to one another, "Even the wind and the sea obey Him!"

As the calm returned, the disciples felt both awe and wonder. They realized that Jesus' power was greater than anything they had ever known. The storm had taught them an important lesson: no matter how big the waves are, they can trust Jesus to keep them safe.

Scripture:

"And he arose, and rebuked the wind, and said unto the sea, Peace, be still. And the wind ceased, and there was a great calm." – Mark 4:39

Questions:

- What was Jesus doing while the storm was happening?
- What did Jesus say to calm the storm?
- How did the disciples feel when they saw the storm obey Jesus?

Phil 4:13 I can do all things through Christ which strengtheneth me.

Phil 4:13 I can do all things through Christ which strengtheneth me.

Jesus Heals a Blind Man

Story:

One day, Jesus saw a man who had been blind since birth. His disciples asked, "Why was this man born blind? Was it because he or his parents sinned?"

Jesus said, "Neither this man nor his parents sinned. He was born blind so God's works could be shown in him."

Jesus spit on the ground, made mud with the dirt, and put it on the man's eyes. Then He told the man, "Go wash in the pool of Siloam." The man obeyed, and when he washed, he could see for the first time in his life!

The man was so happy, and everyone who knew him was amazed. Jesus showed that He is the light of the world and can give both physical and spiritual sight.

The man's neighbors and others who had seen him begged before were astonished. "Isn't this the man who was blind?" they asked. Some believed it was him, while others weren't sure. The man joyfully said, "I am he!" He couldn't wait to share what Jesus had done for him.

Scripture:

"As long as I am in the world, I am the light of the world." – John 9:5

Questions:

- What did Jesus put on the man's eyes to heal him?
- Where did Jesus tell the man to wash?
- What did the man do after he was healed?

Phil 4:13 I can do all things through Christ which strengtheneth me.

Jesus Raises Jairus's Daughter

Story:

A man named Jairus, a leader in the synagogue, came to Jesus. He was very sad and said, "My little daughter is dying. Please come and heal her."

As Jesus went with Jairus, a messenger came and said, "Your daughter is dead. Don't bother the teacher anymore." But Jesus told Jairus, "Don't be afraid; only believe."

When they arrived at Jairus's house, everyone was crying. Jesus said, "Why are you crying? The child is not dead but sleeping." The people laughed because they didn't believe Him.

Jesus went into the room with Jairus and the girl's mother. He took the girl's hand and said, "Little girl, arise." Immediately, she stood up and began walking! Her parents were amazed, and Jesus told them to give her something to eat.

Scripture:

"And he took the damsel by the hand, and said unto her, Talitha cumi; which is, being interpreted, Damsel, I say unto thee, arise." – Mark 5:41

Questions:

- What did Jairus ask Jesus to do for his daughter?
- What did Jesus say to the little girl?
- How did the parents feel after their daughter was raised?

Phil 4:13 I can do all things through Christ which strengtheneth me.

Jesus Heals a Paralyzed Man

Story:

One day, Jesus was teaching in a house. It was so crowded that no one could get inside. Four friends wanted Jesus to heal their paralyzed friend, so they made a hole in the roof and lowered the man on his bed down to Jesus.

When Jesus saw their faith, He said to the man, "Your sins are forgiven." Some people in the crowd thought, "Who can forgive sins but God?"

To show that He had the power to forgive sins, Jesus said to the man, "Rise, take up your bed, and walk." Immediately, the man stood up, picked up his bed, and walked out in front of everyone! The crowd was amazed and praised God.

The paralyzed man's friends were overjoyed as they watched him walk for the first time. They had believed that Jesus could heal him, and their faith had made all the difference. The crowd began to whisper and marvel, saying, "We have never seen anything like this before!" Jesus not only healed the man's body, but He also showed that He has the power to forgive sins—something only God can do. This miracle reminded everyone there that Jesus was truly sent by God and worthy of their trust.

Scripture:

"I say unto thee, Arise, and take up thy bed, and go thy way into thine house." – Mark 2:11

Questions:

- How did the friends get the paralyzed man to Jesus?
- What did Jesus do before healing the man?
- What did the man do after Jesus healed him?

Phil 4:13 I can do all things through Christ which strengtheneth me.

Phil 4:13 I can do all things through Christ which strengtheneth me.

Jesus Fills the Nets with Fish

Story:

One day, Jesus saw some fishermen cleaning their empty nets after fishing all night. Simon Peter was one of the fishermen. Jesus got into Peter's boat and taught the crowd from there.

After teaching, Jesus told Peter, "Go out into the deep water and let down your nets." Peter said, "We fished all night and caught nothing, but if You say so, I'll try again."

When they let down the nets, they caught so many fish that the nets began to break! They called their friends to help, and both boats were so full of fish they almost sank.

Peter was amazed and said, "Lord, I am not worthy to be near You." Jesus said, "Don't be afraid. From now on, you will catch people instead of fish." Peter and his friends left everything and followed Jesus.

Scripture:

"And when they had this done, they inclosed a great multitude of fishes: and their net brake." – Luke 5:6

Questions:

- What did Jesus tell Peter to do with the nets?
- How many fish did they catch?
- What did Peter and his friends do after this miracle?

Phil 4:13 I can do all things through Christ which strengtheneth me.

Jesus Heals Ten Lepers

Story:

As Jesus was traveling to Jerusalem, He passed through a village where ten men with leprosy stood far away. They cried out, "Jesus, Master, have mercy on us!"

Jesus saw them and said, "Go show yourselves to the priests." As they went, they were healed! Their skin became clean, and they were no longer sick.

One of the men, seeing he was healed, turned back and loudly praised God. He fell at Jesus' feet to thank Him. This man was a Samaritan.

Jesus asked, "Were there not ten cleansed? Where are the other nine?" Then He said to the man, "Your faith has made you whole."

Jesus showed that He is kind and powerful, and He loves when we remember to say thank you.

Scripture:

"And one of them, when he saw that he was healed, turned back, and with a loud voice glorified God." – Luke 17:15

Questions:

- How many men did Jesus heal of leprosy?
- How many men came back to thank Jesus?
- What did Jesus say had made the thankful man whole?

Phil 4:13 I can do all things through Christ which strengtheneth me.

Jesus Feeds 4,000 People

Story:

Another time, a large crowd of 4,000 people followed Jesus for three days. They had no food and were very hungry. Jesus told His disciples, "I have compassion on these people and don't want to send them away hungry."

The disciples said, "Where could we get enough food in this remote place?"

Jesus asked, "How many loaves do you have?" They replied, "Seven loaves and a few fish."

Jesus told everyone to sit down. He gave thanks to God and broke the bread and fish into pieces. The disciples handed out the food, and everyone ate until they were full. Afterward, the disciples picked up seven baskets of leftovers!

This miracle showed that Jesus cares for people and has the power to provide for their needs.

Scripture:

"And they did all eat, and were filled: and they took up of the broken meat that was left seven baskets full." – Matthew 15:37

Questions:

- How many days had the crowd been with Jesus?
- How many loaves and fish did the disciples have?
- What did Jesus do before handing out the food?

Phil 4:13 I can do all things through Christ which strengtheneth me.

Jesus Heals a Boy with an Evil Spirit

Story:

A man brought his son to Jesus because the boy was troubled by an evil spirit. The man said, "If You can do anything, please help us."

Jesus said, "If you can believe, all things are possible to those who believe." The man cried out, "Lord, I believe; help my unbelief!"

Jesus commanded the spirit to leave the boy. The spirit left, and the boy was healed! Everyone was amazed at Jesus' power.

Later, the disciples asked, "Why couldn't we cast out the spirit?" Jesus told them, "This kind can only come out by prayer."

Jesus showed that faith and prayer are powerful, and nothing is impossible for Him.

Scripture:

"Jesus said unto him, If thou canst believe, all things are possible to him that believeth." – Mark 9:23

Questions:

- What was wrong with the man's son?
- What did Jesus say is possible for those who believe?
- How did Jesus say the disciples could cast out this kind of spirit?

Phil 4:13 I can do all things through Christ which strengtheneth me.

Phil 4:13 I can do all things through Christ which strengtheneth me.

Jesus Raises Lazarus from the Dead

Story:

Lazarus, a good friend of Jesus, became very sick. His sisters, Mary and Martha, sent a message to Jesus, but Lazarus died before Jesus arrived.

When Jesus came, Martha said, "Lord, if You had been here, my brother would not have died." Jesus said, "Your brother will rise again."

Jesus went to Lazarus's tomb and told the people to roll away the stone. Then Jesus prayed and shouted, "Lazarus, come forth!"

Lazarus came out of the tomb, alive and well, still wrapped in burial clothes! Everyone was amazed.

Jesus showed that He has power over life and death and that we can trust Him even in hard times.

Scripture:

"Jesus said unto her, I am the resurrection, and the life: he that believeth in me, though he were dead, yet shall he live." – John 11:25

Questions:

- What happened to Lazarus before Jesus arrived?
- What did Jesus say to bring Lazarus back to life?
- How do you think Mary and Martha felt when Lazarus came out of the tomb?

Phil 4:13 I can do all things through Christ which strengtheneth me.

Phil 4:13 I can do all things through Christ which strengtheneth me.

Remembering Jesus' Miracles

Water Into Wine

At a wedding in Cana, Jesus turned water into wine when the party ran out, showing His power and care for others.

Who turned water into wine?
What kind of event was Jesus at?
Why did Jesus perform this miracle?

Feeding 5,000 People

With just five loaves of bread and two fish, Jesus fed over 5,000 people, showing He can provide for our needs.

What food did Jesus use to feed the crowd?
How many people ate until they were full?
What did Jesus do before handing out the food?

Walking on Water

Jesus walked on water to meet His disciples during a storm. He reminded them to trust Him, even when afraid.

Who walked on water to meet the disciples?
What happened when Peter became afraid?
What does this miracle teach us about trusting Jesus?

Phil 4:13 I can do all things through Christ which strengtheneth me.

Calming the Storm

Jesus was asleep in a boat during a fierce storm. When His disciples woke Him, He calmed the wind and waves, showing His power over nature.

What did Jesus say to the storm?
How did the disciples feel when the storm stopped?
What does this miracle teach us about faith?

Healing a Blind Man

Jesus healed a man who had been blind since birth by putting mud on his eyes and telling him to wash in the pool of Siloam.

Who healed the blind man?
What did Jesus use to heal his eyes?
What happened when the man obeyed Jesus?

Raising Jairus's Daughter

Jesus raised Jairus's daughter from the dead by taking her hand and saying, "Little girl, arise," showing His power over life.

Who asked Jesus to help his daughter?
What did Jesus say to the little girl?
What happened after Jesus raised her?

Phil 4:13 I can do all things through Christ which strengtheneth me.

Healing a Paralyzed Man

Four friends lowered their paralyzed friend through a roof to see Jesus. Jesus forgave his sins and told him to get up and walk.

How did the friends get the man to Jesus?
What did Jesus say before healing him?
What did the man do after Jesus healed him?

Catching a Big Load of Fish

Jesus told Peter and his friends to cast their nets into the deep water. They caught so many fish that their nets began to break!

What did Jesus tell Peter to do?
How many fish did they catch?
What did Peter and his friends do after this miracle?

Healing Ten Lepers

Jesus healed ten men with leprosy, but only one returned to thank Him, showing the importance of gratitude.

How many men did Jesus heal of leprosy?
How many men came back to thank Jesus?
What did Jesus say to the thankful man?

Feeding 4,000 People

With seven loaves and a few fish, Jesus fed 4,000 people, showing once again that He can provide for us.

How many loaves and fish did Jesus use this time?
How many people were fed?
What did Jesus do before handing out the food?

Healing a Boy with an Evil Spirit

Jesus healed a boy troubled by an evil spirit after his father cried out, "Lord, I believe; help my unbelief!"

Who brought the boy to Jesus?
What did Jesus say about believing?
What happened after Jesus healed the boy?

Raising Lazarus from the Dead

Jesus called Lazarus out of the tomb, bringing him back to life and showing His power over death.

Who did Jesus raise from the dead?
What did Jesus say to bring him out of the tomb?
What does this miracle show about Jesus' power?

This review reminds us of the amazing miracles Jesus did during his earthly ministry and the many lives he touched while doing so.

Phil 4:13 I can do all things through Christ which strengtheneth me.

www.ingramcontent.com/pod-product-compliance
Ingram Content Group UK Ltd.
Pitfield, Milton Keynes, MK11 3LW, UK
UKHW021959140225
455059UK00010B/302